Extreme
SNOW-
BOARDING

Virginia Loh-Hagan

45th Parallel Press

Published in the United States of America by Cherry Lake Publishing
Ann Arbor, Michigan
www.cherrylakepublishing.com

Content Adviser: Liv Williams, Editor, www.iLivExtreme.com
Reading Adviser: Marla Conn, ReadAbility, Inc.
Photo Credits: ©Samot/Shutterstock.com, cover, 1; ©Sergey23/Shutterstock.com, 5; ©NatalieJean/Shutterstock.com, 6; ©Accent Alaska.com/Alamy, 9; ©Nikittta/Dreamstime.com, 11; ©David Spurdens/Thinkstock.com, 12; ©Maxim Blinkov/Shutterstock.com, 14; ©Bikeriderlondon/Shutterstock.com, 17; ©Dudarev Mikhail/Shutterstock.com, 19; ©Vladimir Danilov/Dreamstime.com, 21; ©EvrenKalinbacak/Shutterstock.com, 23; ©Timofeev Sergey/Shutterstock.com, 25; ©Stas Tolstnev/Shutterstock.com, 26; ©Ben Blankenburg/Thinkstock.com, 29; ©Trusjom/Shutterstock.com, multiple interior pages; ©Kues/Shutterstock.com, multiple interior pages

45th Parallel Press is an imprint of Cherry Lake Publishing.

Library of Congress Cataloging-in-Publication Data

Loh-Hagan, Virginia.
 Extreme snowboarding / Virginia Loh-Hagan.
   pages cm. -- (Nailed It!)
 Includes bibliographical references and index.
  ISBN 978-1-63470-018-4 (hardcover) -- ISBN 978-1-63470-072-6 (pdf) -- ISBN 978-1-63470-045-0 (paperback) -- ISBN 978-1-63470-099-3 (ebook)
 1. Snowboarding--Juvenile literature. 2. Extreme sports--Juvenile literature. 3. ESPN X-Games--Juvenile literature. I. Title.

 GV857.S57L65 2015
 796.939--dc23
                   2015006305

ABOUT THE AUTHOR

Dr. Virginia Loh-Hagan is an author, university professor, former classroom teacher, and curriculum designer. She doesn't like the snow or cold. She'd rather be watching TV in her warm house. She lives in San Diego with her very tall husband and very naughty dogs. To learn more about her, visit www.virginialoh.com.

Table of Contents

No Limits!

Who is Ayumu Hirano? Who is Shaun White? Who is Chris Klug? Why are they good examples of extreme snowboarders?

Extreme snowboarders **shred** no matter what. Shred means to snowboard hard and fast.

Ayumu Hirano hit the edge of the **half-pipe**. The half-pipe is a U-shaped ramp. He fell 22 feet (6.7 meters). He hit the bottom. He crashed hard. His helmet cracked. He got back up. He was sore. But he was not scared. He got big air. He won!

Hirano doesn't let age stop him. He won a silver medal in the X Games. He was 14 years old. The X Games are a contest for extreme sports. He also won silver in the Olympics.

Shaun White is "The Flying Tomato." He has red hair. He's fast! He won two Olympic gold medals. He won the most X Games medals.

Extreme snowboarders like to get big air.
They like to go high.

Extreme snowboarders shred hard. They also fall hard.

Voice from the Field: Amy Purdy

Amy Purdy is a double-amputee. At 19, she lost both her legs below the knee. She learned to accept her reality. But she did not accept her limitations. She built her own fake legs. She was snowboarding seven months later. Amy Purdy said, "My legs haven't disabled me, if anything they've enabled me. They've forced me to rely on my imagination and to believe in the possibilities, and that's why I believe that our imaginations can be used as tools for breaking through borders, because in our minds, we can do anything and we can be anything." Watch Amy Purdy's TED Talk titled "Living Beyond Limits" at www.ted.com/talks/amy_purdy_living_beyond_limits.

He had heart problems. He had them since birth. He had three heart operations. White said, "I was supposed to have a 'sluggish heart' and not be able to do much. And here I am." He refused to be limited.

He's not afraid of getting hurt. He fell. He hit the top of a half-pipe. His head snapped back. His helmet flew off. His chin got cut. He sprained a finger. Falling is part of snowboarding.

Chris Klug needed a new liver. He waited six years. He had a **transplant**. This is an operation to get a new organ. Four days later, he left the hospital. He snowboarded again. He won a World Cup award. He won a bronze medal. He's the first transplant **recipient** to win an Olympic medal. A recipient receives, or gets, something.

Nothing stops Klug. He said, "I'm going to keep challenging myself." He wants to complete the Seven **Summits**. These are the highest mountains on each of the seven continents. Summit means to reach the top. He'll be the first transplant recipient to do this.

Extreme snowboarders do not see limitations. They see opportunities to do the impossible.

"I'm going to keep challenging myself."

Chris Klug has won many snowboarding awards. He wants to do the Seven Summits.

No Brakes!

How can extreme snowboarders stop their snowboards? What gear do snowboarders need? What happened when snowboarders were banned from ski resorts?

Extreme snowboarders ride the steepest slopes. They rip the deepest snow. Rip means to cut through. They do it without **brakes**. To brake is to stop. They brake by leaning back. They brake by turning their boards. They turn them to the side.

They learned how to stop their boards. But they can't stop their imaginations. Chloe Kim flew 14 feet (4.2 m) above a 22-foot (6.7 m) wall. She's the youngest person to win a gold medal. She competed in the X Games. She was 14 years old.

Snowboarders need a board, boots, and **bindings**. Bindings hold the boots in place.

Snowboarders were **banned** from ski resorts. They weren't allowed to be there. Skiers were afraid of crashing. They were hurt by runaway boards.

The bans didn't stop snowboarders. They went to the **backcountry** instead. Backcountry means undeveloped

There are different boots and boards depending on the type of snowboarding.

The wild nature of the backcountry brings a challenge at every turn.

places. They ride down hills leading to rivers. They ride off trails. They ride on uneven **terrain**, or land. They jump off **obstacles**. Obstacles are things used to get air. Obstacles include rocks, trees, gaps, or cliffs. Obstacles are fun. But they can be dangerous. Snowboarders also learn to avoid them.

Freestyle snowboarders create new tricks. Travis Rice is very daring. He jumped a 120-foot (36.5 m) gap in Utah.

Extreme Snowboarding: Know the Lingo

Bail: to crash land

Big air: high, long jump

Fakie: riding backward

Gnarly: beyond rad, beyond extreme, perfection; dangerous

Goofy: left foot on tail, right foot on nose

Grommet: talented young snowboarder

Huck: flying wildly in the air on a board and then crashing

Ollie: springing off the tail of the board and into the air

Rad: cool, radical

Run: going from top to bottom; includes obstacles and tricks

Shred: hard, fast snowboarding

Sick: really awesome

Sketching: nearly falling as you ride

Spin masters: snowboarders who pull off smooth turns in the air

Stick: snowboard

Wipeout: falling or crashing

There are many different moves and tricks.

He was the first to land a 1080. This is three full turns. He said, "Adventure is what you make of it."

Downhill snowboarding is another type of extreme snowboarding. Snowboarders look for tall mountains. They get to the top. Some use climbing gear. Some drop from helicopters. They focus on speed. It's dangerous. The terrain is rough.

They look for steep slopes. They like to catch big air. They show off their skills. They like to do **inverted aerials**. Inverted means upside down. Aerials are tricks in the air.

They combine moves. They create new tricks. Tricks have interesting names. Some examples include Spaghetti Air, Canadian Bacon, and Hot Garbage.

"Adventure is what you make of it."

Respect the Mountain

What are some dangers caused by mountain weather? What is an avalanche? What are some dangers of snowboarding?

Mountain weather can be dangerous. Extreme snowboarders face strong winds. They face below-freezing temperatures. It may be cold. But they can still get a sunburn. The sun reflects off the snow.

Weather is **unpredictable**. No one knows what's going to happen. Sunshine can turn into a storm. **Avalanches** are very dangerous. It's when snow flows quickly down a slope. All snowboarders should have **beacons**. Beacons give off signals. Rescuers get the signals. They find people buried under snow.

An avalanche killed Liz Daley. She was snowboarding. The avalanche carried her over a cliff. Marguerite Cossettini survived two avalanches. She helped dig three people out.

Extreme snowboarders respect the mountain. Anything could happen.

Extreme snowboarders can get hurt. They've fallen off cliffs and gaps. They've hit deep snow, rocks, and trees.

Sluffs and slabs are two types of avalanches. A sluff is dry, powdery snow. Expert snowboarders can ride sluff.

CLOSED AVALANCHE DANGER

Getting Your Body Ready

Many extreme snowboarders take avalanche safety classes. It's best to rescue an avalanche victim within 15 minutes. Then they have a 90 percent chance of survival. Snowboarders need to practice digging in the snow.

☞ If you're in an avalanche, do the following: Jump up the slope. Move to the side of the avalanche. Let go of gear except for safety gear. Hold on to something. Swim to the surface. Swim on your back and swim uphill.

☞ If you get buried, do the following: Hold one arm straight above your head. Spit to see which way is up. Dig an air pocket around your face. (This gives you 30 minutes of breathing time.) Save air and energy.

They get sprains. They hurt ankles, knees, and wrists. Head injuries are common. Most injuries are from falling on hard ice.

Kevin Pearce won many medals. He had a snowboarding accident. He got a **traumatic** brain injury. Traumatic

Extreme snowboarding can be dangerous. Snowboarders can get hurt.

means serious. It happened two months before the Olympics. He was training. He tried to land a difficult trick. He fell. His head hit the ice. He spent many days in a coma.

From Snurfer to Snowboard

How did snowboards develop? Who created the early snowboards?

Some extreme athletes love surfing and skateboarding. They transferred the same skills to snowboarding. Snowboarding developed from nothing to an Olympic sport.

Early boards were used in 1850. They were used in Turkey. It's a country in Europe. People used wooden tablets as boards. They traveled between villages.

In 1929, M. J. Burchett created one of the first boards. He cut a wooden plank. He connected it to clotheslines. He also used horse **reins**. Reins are ropes used to control horses.

Vern Wicklund built a sled. He was 13 years old. In 1939, he worked with Harvey and Gunnar Burgeson. They invented a board. They called it a bunker. It wasn't a success. They only made five.

Sherman Poppen was an American surfer. He made a board in 1966. He watched his daughter playing. She was sledding

Extreme snowboarders copied skateboarding tricks and moves.

while standing up. Poppen put two skis together. He attached a rope at the front. His wife called it a snurfer. This stands for snow surfer. He sold nearly a million snurfers. Poppen organized snurfing contests. Tom Sims and Jake Burton Carpenter liked snurfing. They improved the snurfer.

NAILED IT!

When Extreme Is Too Extreme!

Trevor Jacob jumped over a moving train! The train passed by a gap in the trees. He came down the mountain. The train came. He jumped over the train. He landed on the other side. Jacob has wanted to do this stunt since he was 5 years old. His friend said, "That kid's crazy." Jacob was inspired by Andy Hetzel and Temple Cummins. They were the first snowboarders to jump a moving train. The stunt is called the Donner Pass Train Jump. It's near Lake Tahoe.

Better boards moved the sport from powder surfing to real snowboarding.

Carpenter started Burton Boards. He attached water ski bindings. This changed snowboarding for the better. Boards were easier to control.

Sims made a "ski board" in eighth grade. He combined skiing and skateboarding. He started Sims Snowboards and Skateboards. He added metal edges. These boards can be used on hard slopes.

"This changed snowboarding for the better."

Snowboarders
Are Explorers!

What is adventure-based snowboarding? Who are Xavier de Le Rue and Lucas Debari? Who is Jeremy Jones?

Extreme snowboarders want to be first. They want to be first to do a trick. They want to be first to go down a slope. They travel to remote, or faraway, places.

Xavier de Le Rue and Lucas Debari went to Antarctica. They couldn't call for help. They were by themselves. They spent a month there.

They climbed mountains for hours. They snowboarded down. The slopes had never been ridden before. They had no information about the slopes. They learned as they explored. The terrain was rough. There were dangerous ice slabs. Mistakes could mean death.

This is called "adventure-based snowboarding." It's more than just snowboarding. It's exploring!

Jeremy Jones looks for steep mountains. He looks for bodies of water. He looks for wet and sticky snow. He studies his locations. He studies maps. He talks to local people. He studies avalanches.

Extreme snowboarders create their own adventures.

Snowboarders explore their mountains.

He learns the most from exploring. He drags supplies uphill on sleds. He sets up camps. He sleeps in cold temperatures. He walks in waist-high snow. He snowboards down slopes. He jumps over huge rocks. He makes sharp turns. He rolls. He falls into snow. But he always gets up.

NAILED IT!

That Happened?!?

June Mountain is near June Lake, California. The city hosted a snowboarding contest. The contest was the 1989 OP Pro competition. They built a half-pipe for the contest. They needed to build vertical walls. The walls needed to go straight up. They used bundles of hay. They stacked the hay. They covered the hay with snow. Snowboarders went up and down the half-pipe. Then smoke came out of the snow. The hay had caught on fire! The fire melted holes in the snow. Smoke came out of black holes. That didn't stop the snowboarders. They kept going.

Jones said, "I still make mistakes and am always trying to gain as much mountain knowledge as possible."

Travis Rice has no fear. He explores places no one has been. He snowboarded in South America. He explored 300 miles (483 kilometers) of the Andes Mountains. He takes risks.

Rice did aerial tricks. This is dangerous to do in unknown places. He could have tumbled down a mountain wall. He could have fallen into a gap. Rice said, "You have to ride smart …You have to know when to go for it and when to pull back …You have to see opportunity when it knocks on your door."

Extreme snowboarders like to do tricks in the air.

Did You Know?

- Thomas Murphy tried to escape an avalanche. He jumped off several steep cliffs. His last leap knocked him out. He woke up in the dark. He was trapped in the snow. He was at a height of 5,000 feet (1,524 m). He used his cell phone. He called for rescue. He also called his family. He didn't think he'd make it. A rescue helicopter came. He waved his phone. The pilot spotted the light. He was saved by his cell phone.

- Stefan Gatt climbed up Mount Everest. It's the world's tallest peak. He did it without bottled oxygen. He also carried his own equipment. He was the first to snowboard down part of the mountain.

- Šárka Pančochová is from the Czech Republic. She competed in the 2014 Winter Olympics. She fell while trying to land a jump. Her head hit the slope. It was the worst crash of the competition. Her helmet saved her from a major head injury. She crashed so hard that her helmet cracked.

- Wind snowboarding is another version of extreme snowboarding. Wind snowboarders attach sails to snowboards. They let the wind pull them across slopes. This means they go really fast.

- Craig Kelly was a professional snowboarder. He died on January 20, 2003. He was trapped by an avalanche. The avalanche trapped eight people and killed six others. Kelly is known as the "godfather of freeriding." He said, "When I want to be happy, I go snowboarding."

Consider This!

TAKE A POSITION! Snowboarder Chris Klug got his liver from a 13-year-old boy. The boy was accidentally shot to death. The boy's organs saved two other people. Organ donation saved Klug's life. Some people do not agree with donating organs. What do you think about organ donations? Argue your point with reasons and evidence.

SAY WHAT? Extreme snowboarding is a combination of other extreme sports. It especially copies a lot from skateboarding. Most snowboarders practice skateboarding in spring and summer. Explain how extreme snowboarding is influenced by other extreme sports.

THINK ABOUT IT! Snowboarding wasn't included in the Olympics until 1998. Why do you think it took people a while to accept snowboarding as a sport?

SEE A DIFFERENT SIDE! Imagine you're skiing at a resort. You almost get hit by a runaway snowboard. How would you feel? Now imagine you are very excited to go snowboarding. But when you get to the mountain, snowboarding is banned. How would you feel then? Talk about these different perspectives with a friend.

Learn More: Resources

Primary Sources

The Art of Flight, a documentary about snowboarder Travis Rice and friends (directed by Curt Morgan, 2011), www.artofflightmovie.com

Chris Klug's history, www.chrisklug.com/history. html (Klug also wrote a book with Steve Jackson titled *To the Edge and Back: My Story from Organ Transplant Survivor to Olympic Snowboarder.*)

Secondary Sources

Fitzpatrick, Jim. *Snowboarding.* Ann Arbor, MI: Cherry Lake Publishing, 2009.

Hayhurst, Chris. *Snowboarding! Shred the Powder.* New York: Rosen Publishing Group, 1999.

Woods, Bob. *Snowboarding.* Milwaukee, WI: Gareth Stevens, 2004.

Web Sites

National Ski and Board Safety Association: http://safe2skiandboard.org

United States of America Snowboard and Freeski Association: https://www.usasa.org

X Games—Snowboarding: http://xgames.espn.go.com/snowboarding/

Glossary

aerials (AIR-ee-uhlz) tricks in the air

avalanches (AV-uh-lanch-iz) when snow flows quickly down a slope

backcountry (BAK-kun-tree) natural or undeveloped places

banned (BAND) not allowed

beacons (BEE-kunz) devices that signal location

bindings (BINDE-ingz) devices that hold boots in place

brakes (BRAKES) devices that help you slow down or stop

half-pipe (HAF-pipe) a U-shaped ramp

inverted (in-VUR-ted) upside down

obstacles (OB-stuh-kuhlz) things used to get air, like rocks, trees, cliffs, or ramps

recipient (rih-SIP-ee-uhnt) a person who receives, or gets, something

reins (RAYNZ) ropes that control horses

shred (SHRED) snowboarding hard and fast

summits (SUM-its) high peaks; to climb a high peak

terrain (tuh-RAYN) land

transplant (TRANS-plant) an operation to get a new organ

traumatic (traw-MAH-tik) serious and damaging

unpredictable (un-pree-DIK-tuh-buhl) not able to know what's going to happen

Index